Penny Stocks

How To Start Trading Penny Stocks

Alvin Williams

regarding its prolonged validity or interim quality. Trademarks that are mentioned are done without written consent and can in no way be considered an endorsement from the trademark holder.

CONTENTS

Introduction 1

Chapter 1: Understanding Penny Stocks 2

Chapter 2: Risks and Benefits 15

Chapter 3: Best Trading Practices 25

Chapter 4: Start Trading 41

Chapter 5: Common Pitfalls and How to Avoid Them 59

Conclusion 69

Introduction

Congratulations on downloading this book and thank you for doing so.

The following chapters will discuss everything you need to know about penny stocks, and how you can become a successful trader. You will learn what penny stocks are, how to identify the best penny stocks to invest in, as well as the common pitfalls that you should be aware of, and more!

There are plenty of books on this subject on the market, thanks again for choosing this one! Every effort was made to ensure it is full of as much useful information as possible, please enjoy!

Chapter 1: Understanding Penny Stocks

As discussed in the first book, penny stocks are stocks that have a value of less than $5 per share. In the United Kingdom, any stock that costs less than £1 is considered a penny stock. Penny stocks are also referred to as cent stocks or penny shares.

Because penny stocks have a relatively low value, they are mostly traded by small and start-up companies. However, you can still find a few big and well-established companies that trade penny stocks on major market exchanges.

Trading penny stocks vs. gambling

Some people think that trading penny stocks is similar to gambling, for good reasons: First, the high volatility of penny stocks can be likened to a game of slots in a casino where you can quickly lose your money or earn a big amount within a short period of time. Second, with so many factors that affect the prices of penny stocks, these stocks have a highly speculative value — just like casino games, which are very speculative. Last but not least, majority of people who invest in penny stocks lose their money, which is the normal state of things in the casino.

However...

Unlike casino games, the outcome of every trade does not come from a shuffled deck of cards or a mere random generator. Every result is caused by the market movement, which comes from real people and businesses. Therefore, unlike a game of slots where you depend on pure luck to earn money, trading penny slots lets you examine economic indicators and other factors that greatly influence the outcome of any trade. This means that if you know the proper way to approach every trade that you make, if you know the right strategies to use and have the correct data to analyze, you can significantly increase your chances of success by more than 80%.

Of course, if you do not exert any serious effort or research and simply trade penny stocks by merely relying on pure luck, then you are gambling. But, if you want to be a professional trader and make a living trading penny stocks - if you are willing to spend hours of research and study to analyze the market movement and identify the best stocks - then that is not gambling but investing.

Is trading penny stocks for you?

Penny stocks have a high volatility. Their prices can fluctuate dramatically within a short period of time, and such changes in their prices are considered normal. On the one hand, the high volatility of penny stocks can cause a penny stock that has a value of $3 today to have a value of less than a dollar in the next few days. On the other hand, such high volatility of penny stocks can make them double, triple, or even increase their value to more than 15 times in just a short period of time.

As the saying goes: "The higher the risk, the higher the return." In the same manner, the lower the risk, the lower is the return. Trading penny stocks is considered a high-risk investment, counterbalanced by its high-profit potential. If you do not want a high-risk investment, you might do well with blue-chip stocks. However, the return will also be lower. But, if you do not mind the risk, if you want to grow your investment to more than thrice its value within a short period of time, then trading penny stocks could be the best decision you can ever make.

If you have more than enough funds available, you can get the best of both worlds by investing a part of your funds in penny stocks and applying the rest to buy some blue-chip stocks.

Penny stocks vs. blue-chip stocks

Penny stocks and blue-chip stocks are issued by companies. Although both are considered stocks, there are significant differences between the two.

Volatility

Unlike penny stocks, blue-chip stocks have low volatility. This means that their prices do not usually fluctuate as much, which makes them very stable. However, such low volatility also means having a low-profit potential.

Sensitivity

Sector influences easily affect the prices of penny stocks, which is one of the reasons why penny shares are very volatile. Blue-chip stocks are more stable and are not easily affected by sector influences.

Profit potential

On the one hand, to earn a lot with blue-chip stocks, you will have to invest more money. Although investing in blue-chip stocks is more secure, the profit potential is also low. A 50% increase is already considered high. On the other hand, investing in penny stocks has a much higher profit potential. An increase of 50% is considered normal. In fact, if you get really lucky, the value of your penny stocks can increase by more than 20 times.

Speculative

Blue-chip stocks have little to no speculative value, while the value of penny stocks is very speculative. There are so many factors that affect the prices of penny stocks, and many of which are outside your control.

Dividends

If you are a holder of blue-chip stocks, then you can expect to receive dividends from the company. However, if you are a holder of penny stocks, you would barely receive any dividends.

Availability of data

The information that you can get when you research about penny stocks is limited. Penny stocks are not as transparent as blue-chip stocks. This makes their value harder to speculate. Blue-chip stocks are more open and transparent. Many companies reveal their books and financial data, which can help you gauge if the company is doing well or not.

Penny stock volatility

If there is one thing that penny stocks are known for, it is their high volatility. If you take a look at the penny stock market, you will notice that huge price swings are normal, and they happen within a short period of time.

But, what does *volatility* mean? Volatility means quick and unpredictable changes. Hence, when we say that penny stocks have high volatility, it means that their prices change dramatically and rapidly.

The high volatility of penny stocks cuts both ways:

- Their high volatile nature makes their prices difficult to predict; therefore, you can easily lose money by investing in the wrong penny shares.

- Their high volatility is what causes the big price swings; therefore, there is a good opportunity to earn a big profit.

Before you start trading, it is important for you to know the causes behind the high volatility of penny stocks by looking at the factors that strongly affect their prices:

Traders themselves

Every time a trader buys or sells a penny stock, it has an impact on the price movement of the stock concerned. Traders, of course, have their own preferences as to when to buy or sell their stocks, including which penny stocks they will buy or sell; and this is something that you cannot control.

Volatile nature

When you deal with penny stocks, you need to realize that you do not just deal with stocks or graphs that you see on the computer. Instead, you deal with real people and businesses. The market is volatile in nature because it is alive. Therefore, you can expect continuous changes to take place.

Consumer behavior

For any business to succeed, it all depends on consumer behavior. The consumers are the main customers of a business (except, of course, in the case of a B-to-B enterprise). But every consumer has his own preferences and prejudices, and they also change. A product that is happily accepted by the market today may be completely forgotten tomorrow.

Government laws and policies

Governments have an active interest in businesses. In fact, they even enact laws to encourage investors to make an investment. Of course, they also gain benefits from businesses, such as being able to provide employment to their citizens, as well as the money that they receive from taxes. Government laws and policies affect the volatility of penny stocks because their laws can directly affect businesses. They exercise a strong influence over businesses and investors, and can even direct market behavior.

Economic problems

When the economy is not doing well, businesses also fail to make a good profit. This usually results in a significant decrease in the prices of penny stocks. This is one of the reasons why economic problems should be resolved at the first instance. Economic problems will not just pull down the values of various penny stocks, but can also adversely affect the lives of the people.

Reports

Financial reports of publicly-traded companies are released periodically. These reports are open to the public, and traders use them to find out the best penny stocks to invest in. However, it is worth noting that although these reports are good factors to be considered, they are not sufficient to guarantee the success of a trade. Still, when these reports are released, they tend to influence the decisions of many investors, which affect the volatility of stocks.

Competition

Competition is good for consumers because it compels businesses to only offer the best quality of products and services. Competition can also be beneficial to businesses by compelling them to improve and grow. However, as one business wins against its competitors and increases the value of its stocks, this diminishes the value of the stocks of its competitors. This, of course, will affect the prices of penny stocks in the market.

These factors, among others, greatly influence the prices of penny stocks, which explains the high volatility of the penny stock market. This makes the prices of penny stocks difficult to predict with certainty. Not only are there many factors to consider, but even a single element has a potential to create a significant change in the prices of penny stocks.

Take advantage of price swings

Although the high volatility of penny stocks is what discourages some investors, it is also this same reason that makes it an attractive investment. It is the dramatic price swings that will enable you to double, triple, or even multiply your investment by more than 20 times.

Although you can trade penny stocks within a single day, it is not uncommon to see traders who wait for days or weeks before they sell their stocks. Since high volatility is a major characteristic of penny stocks, you can expect their value to rise. Unfortunately, there is also a probability that their value may drop significantly.

Chapter 2: Risks and Benefits

There are two things that trading penny stocks are very much known for:

1. You can quickly make a big amount of money.

2. There is a high probability that you will lose your investment.

These are two opposing extremes that you will be facing. Of course, your objective is to rake in serious profits. Unfortunately, the majority of people who trade penny stocks fail to make any positive return. In fact, they lose their money. But do not be discouraged; because there are still people out there, the well-experienced and real expert traders who double, triple, and continuously grow their money more than you can ever imagine.

Losing a trade is normal. Even well-experienced traders make the wrong investment decisions from time to time. However, you must avoid such mistakes as much as possible. Now, in order to help cut down your future losses, you should be aware of the risks that you will be facing when you trade penny stocks.

The risks

Small companies

The majority of the companies in the penny stock market are small companies. In fact, they can be so small that they do not even meet the minimum capitalization requirement. You will find many of these companies on the Pink Sheets. But then again, as discussed in the previous book, do not buy penny stocks from the Pink Sheets. Since they are small companies, it is hard to tell if they are stable enough and if they will even grow. Many small companies also tend to be less professional. Sometimes the executives of a small company see and treat the assets of the company, including the stocks and penny shares, as their own personal belonging.

Start-up companies

Many of the companies that issue penny stocks are the start-up companies. Therefore, they tend to have a very limited history that you can track. This makes it risky because you would not know for sure if the business is legitimate or if the company is operating a scam.

Less transparent

Penny stocks do not have stringent requirements. You can always buy them on the Pink Sheets or over the counter (OTC). Remember that the companies on the Pink Sheets are not required to file with the SEC and to meet the minimum capitalization requirements or capital stock of a legitimate company.

Many companies on the Pink Sheets only reveal very limited information about their business, so it is hard to get sufficient and accurate data. Worse, some companies operate a scam.

Bankruptcy

The penny stock market is not only participated by small and start-up companies, it also has companies that are about to go bankrupt. Unfortunately, these struggling companies will not reveal that they are already about to declare bankruptcy and will even make their stocks to look like an attractive investment. Of course, there is still a probability to make a good amount of profit when you invest in a company that is struggling to survive, especially when the company is able to save itself from bankruptcy and begin to grow successfully. However, the probability for such ideal scenario to happen is small. Trading penny stocks is already risky enough; you would not want to take more risks.

The reason why you should not invest in a company that is about to go bankrupt is because you will run the risk of losing everything. Once the company declares bankruptcy and does not have sufficient assets to cover all its debts and obligations to its creditors, you will not be able to get your money back.

Low liquidity

Penny stocks have low liquidity. With a low liquidity, they become open to manipulation. A common type of fraudulent scheme is the pump and dump, in which the value of certain penny stocks are pumped up using some fraudulent marketing hype in order to convince traders to buy them. As its name already implies, the price of certain stocks are pumped up using some promotional or marketing hype. In turn, traders will find the stocks attractive and make an investment. The penny stocks are then dumped on the traders and their value begins to fall down.

Take note that the pump and dump scheme can be applied even if the company is actually doing well. In fact, when the company is making profits, the pump and dump scheme will be harder to detect. By adding a few dollars on the price of certain stocks that are already increasing, it is almost impossible for traders to determine whether the increased total value is due to legitimate means or merely a result of a pump and dump scheme.

Speculative

Due to so many factors that affect the prices of penny stocks, it can be said that the penny stock market is highly speculative. An important thing in trading penny stocks is to first buy the stocks that truly have a good value. Unfortunately, with the increasing number of scams, hackers, and frauds out there, it becomes difficult to know whether you are really purchasing a good stock or merely a stock whose value is being pumped. Second, even if you get to buy a profitable stock, there are many active factors that can affect its performance in the market. The best stock today may no longer be considered a good stock by tomorrow, depending on the circumstances.

Also, granting that the prices of your penny stocks increase, will the buyers still see them attractive and profitable by the time you want to sell them?

These, among many other things, are the risks faced by traders of penny stocks. Consider also the sad fact that most traders fail to make any profit and simply lose their investment.

Do you think you are up for the challenge? If your entrepreneurial spirit is not crushed by these risks, then get ready for the awesome benefits of trading penny stocks.

The Benefits

Trading penny stocks is one of the best investment opportunities that offer wonderful benefits. So, if you honestly think that you can manage the above mentioned risks, then welcome to the world of high profits — a place where you can double, triple, or even multiply your money by more than 20 times in a short period of time.

Price

Penny stocks are cheap. A single penny stock only costs less than $5. If you have a lot of money to invest, then you can have thousands of stocks of different companies. If you are on a shoestring budget, then this opportunity is also available to you.

High potential return

When you trade penny stocks, there is a potential to multiply the value of your stocks many times over. In fact, there is a potential for the prices of your stocks to double within 24 hours or less.

Unlike blue-chip stocks where a 60% increase is considered a big profit already, such is considered normal when you trade penny stocks. And, unlike binary options where you can gain 90% but has a much higher risk, trading penny stocks can make your money grow by more than 500% within a short period of time. Also, since the penny stock market is mostly composed of small businesses, there is a high probability for the value of their penny stocks to grow, since small businesses have a lot of space for improvements.

High volume

You can have thousands of penny stocks for a small amount. Having a high volume of penny stocks is good, especially if you get them from a start-up company that is doing well.

Low or controlled risk

Penny stocks are inexpensive. You do not have to purchase a lot of penny stocks to earn a decent amount of profit. You can also diversify your stocks to help minimize your losses. And, unlike trading binary options where you will lose your whole wager when you make a wrong investment decision, you can still keep your penny stocks and sell them. If you are patient enough, there is really no such thing as a permanent loss. Considering the volatility of penny stocks, even if the value of your penny stocks decreases, there is a good chance that it will increase after some time.

Chapter 3: Best Trading Practices

No matter what strategy you use, there are best practices that all experienced and successful traders observe. These are the keys that will help you succeed. These things are not just something that you read because their true essence is in doing, so be sure to apply them to your every trade. Here are the best trading practices that you should know:

Do your research

Do not simply focus on the penny stocks that you want to purchase. Keep in mind that the performance of stocks heavily depends upon the overall performance of the business. Therefore, you must also give attention to the company itself. How is the company doing in the market? Does it match up well against its competitors? Remember to research the penny stocks that you intend to purchase, as well as the company concerned.

The scope of research is, if course, a big task. This is one of the most important parts of trading. Also find out the factors that affect a particular stock and understand them. Are these factors present at the current moment? Is there any chance that any of these influential factors appear in the future? If so, what are the consequences? The more research and knowledge that you have the better is your chances of investing in the right penny stocks.

Only invest the money you can afford to lose

A very common advice known to all gamblers is this: "Only play with the money you can afford to lose." This is a common advice given to gamblers. Although trading penny stocks may not be considered gambling, especially if you do not rely on pure luck, it is still similar to gambling in the sense that there is always the possibility to lose your money. Do not use the money that you need for your child's enrollment or for paying the household bills, etc. Although there is no assurance that you will lose you money, you must only invest the money that you can afford to lose. The penny stock market is very volatile that it is hard to guarantee that you will make a profit.

Set a limit

It is a sound advice, especially for beginners, to decide before making any trade on a limit on how long will you continue to hold on to a losing stock, as well as for a profitable one. The penny stock market is extremely volatile. Although you can expect for their value to increase and decrease almost randomly, it does not always mean that a stock whose price has just decreased will soon increase.

Part of the volatility of penny stocks is that a significant decrease in value can still be followed by another big drop. Therefore, in order to cut down your losses, it is important to set a limit on how long would you be willing to hold on to a losing stock. In the same way, you should know how long you will hold on to a winning stock. Again, even if a stock continuously experiences an increase in value, there is still the possibility that its price can just drop dramatically, almost without any warning.

Look for patterns

The movement of the prices of penny stocks can be said to be like random. The thing is, randomness creates patterns. And, if it is not random, then there is more possibility to find a pattern. If you can identify these patterns early, then you will be one step ahead. Just remember, though, that patterns are like trends; and in the world of penny stocks, they do not last for very long.

Observe the trends

Analyze the graphs and tables that show the performance of certain penny stocks. Do not just study their current record, but also check their past performance. This is a good way for you to know if the stocks are really doing well or not. Also, do not rely completely on the latest trends. Although the latest trends can show you the most recent performances of penny stocks, you must take note that trends often change. In fact, in the penny stock market, you will barely see a trend that will last for too long.

Know the latest news

If you are serious about trading penny stocks, then you should be updated on the latest news. The many factors that affect the prices of penny stocks are usually revealed on the news. Although the news would not state it directly, you should know that laws, businesses, economy, market behavior, and inflation, among others, can affect the prices of penny stocks. Take note, however, that although the news can give you valuable insights and information, what matters the most is still the actual prices of penny stocks.

Stay calm

Bad days do happen, and you may encounter a series of losing streaks despite doing some good research. During such moment, or the moment when you first experience your first loss, stay calm. I repeat: stay calm. The penny stock market does not care about how you feel, so must remain objective and focused. If you cannot control yourself, just quickly turn off your computer or mobile phone.

Do not be greedy

Especially for beginners, it is recommended that you stick to getting small yet regular profits. Many inexperienced traders lose their money not because of buying the wrong penny stocks, but because of keeping the stocks for too long. Do not underestimate the high volatile nature of the penny stock market. Learn to sell, cash out, and enjoy your profit.

Keep your emotion under control

Do not be an emotional trader. Although it is good to feel passionate about trading penny stocks, do not let your passion blind your judgment. Never make any trade when under pressure and treat trading penny stocks as a business.

Make your own decision

Although it is advisable to read the opinions of "experts," it is wrong to let them dictate your investment decisions. Unfortunately, many of these so-called "experts" are hacks and frauds. They promote themselves as an expert even if their overall losses outweigh their profits. Of course, there are still a few real experts out there, but even the best traders still commit mistakes from time to time. After all, the process of developing your trading strategy is a life-long journey.

Instead of relying on expert advice, you should develop your own understanding of the penny stock market and make your own decisions. You can compare your decisions with the pieces of advice given by "experts" and see how well you match up. Of course, you also need to check the real outcome of a particular trade to see if you have made the right investment decision.

Do not chase after your losses

This is another advice given to gamblers. Unfortunately, although this advice is very common, many still fail to observe it. There are several ways to chase after your losses, but they all usually lead to the same unfortunate result. Usually, you chase after your losses by investing more right after you lose a trade. When you lose, you simply have this strong urge to get your money back. Another thing people do is by continuously holding on to losing stocks, thinking that once they sell them, they would no longer save their lost investment. In any way, you are on the losing side with just a little hope of getting your losses back. The bad thing here is that you gamble your whole funds for the sake of recovering a few losses. Therefore, the risk is really high.

A good way to avoid this is by learning to accept your losses. If certain penny stocks fail to meet your expectations, learn to accept your losses by selling them and starting over again. When you seriously engage in trading penny stocks, losing some investments is normal. After all, once you get lucky and hit truly profitable stocks, you will quickly recover all your losses and enjoy grand profits.

Stick to your strategy

During the execution process, you must do your best to stick to your planned strategy; otherwise, you will not be able to measure effectiveness, as well as its full potential. Of course, there are instances that you should abandon your strategy, especially if circumstances clearly show that continuing with your strategy will result in a total loss of investment.

Only invest in penny stocks that have a high volume

According to some "expert," you should only invest in stocks that trade at least a hundred thousand shares per day. This serves as a safeguard against the risk of being illiquid.

Pump your stocks

There is a reason why the pump and dump scheme still exists despite many people being aware of such scheme: It works.

So, if you do not mind being a bit tricky, you can market yourself as an "expert" in trading penny stocks. You can put up a website and send out newsletters to your readers. You can then purchase cheap penny stocks, use your connections to gain interest in the stocks, and sell them at a premium price. If you are the type that can convince people to do what you want, then this may be an easy way for you to make money. However, if you are the type who cannot exercise a bit of trickery (which is a very good thing about you), then you can simply take advantage of people who pump and dump their stocks. How? Simply buy their penny stocks, preferably before they pump them or as early as possible while they pump their value. You can then wait for their price to increase, sell your penny stocks, and reap some profits.

Keep a journal

Writing a journal is not required, but it is very helpful. You do not have to be a professional writer to write a journal. What is important is for you to be honest about everything that you write.

There are many things that you can write in your journal. It is also good to write your goals and reasons for why you want to trade penny stocks. Also, write any lessons and mistakes that you have learned. It is your journal, so feel free to write about anything and everything about your trading adventure. A journal will allow you to think outside the box and be a smarter trader.

Take a break

Trading penny stocks has a gambling factor: It can be addicting. It is something that you can do for hours without being tired. You would feel more like playing than working. However, when you engage in research, which is a must, that is the time where you will definitely feel that trading penny stocks involve serious work. Allow yourself to take a break from to time. Remember that you will have a better mental clarity if you give yourself a chance to take a rest.

Get the latest updates quickly

Successful traders get the latest news and respond quickly. The way to take advantage of the impact of the news on the prices of stocks is by making the appropriate trading actions just before others realize them. For example, when you see that your penny stocks will soon encounter a massive drop in value, sell them right away. Also, if possible, know the news before it is even released in the public. To increase the probability that certain stocks will increase in value, the stocks should also be effectively promoted. Therefore, it is helpful if you can join and be active on online groups and forums on penny stocks.

Focus on start-up companies

One of the best things about the penny stock market is that it is a place where you can find many start-up companies. Surely, a good number of these companies will do well. Unfortunately, some of them will perform badly and even get bankrupt. However, if you manage to get the stocks of the good start-up companies early on, you will find yourself in a winning position.

Therefore, you must exert the effort to research and analyze the different start-up companies that participate in the penny stock market. When analyzing a particular company, also measure how it matches up against its competitors in the market.

Growing companies have lots of space for improvements; and as their profits increase and they continue to expand, the prices of their penny stocks also increase.

Have fun

It is a common advice that you should choose a job that you enjoy. In the same way, you should enjoy trading penny stocks. If you do not enjoy it, then maybe it is a signal that you should just invest somewhere else. Also, you can make better decisions when you are having fun.

Choose the right penny stocks

Always choose the right penny stocks to invest in. How do you know the right ones? Sufficient research. Never commence a trade without sufficient research. Take note that a little research is not enough. Researches made without serious efforts are only as good as a mere toss of a coin. Also, the most profitable and attractive-looking stocks may not always be the right penny stocks to invest in. After all, no matter what the media says, the numbers on the penny stock market are what counts.

Be patient

Patience is important when you trade penny stocks. Do not hurry to make a buy order simply because you have funds in your account. Also, many times, to take advantage of the high volatility of penny stocks, you will have to wait for some time. Take note that every action that you make is essential. The stocks that you buy today are the stocks that you will soon sell. Be patient, wait for the proper timing, and act accordingly.

Use the high volatility to your advantage

Although many people shy away from penny stocks due to their high volatility, it is this volatile nature of penny stocks that make them a profitable investment. With high volatility, mastering the famous principle for making money is the key to profit: buy when the price is low, and sell when the price is high.

Chapter 4: Start Trading

The only way to truly understand how to trade penny stocks is by actual application. If you think that you are ready to face the challenges and enjoy the immense benefits of trading penny stocks, then it is time for you to get in the game and make your first trade.

What to look for in a penny stock broker

In order to trade penny stocks, you will need a broker. It is easy to find brokers online. In fact, simply by doing a quick search online you will find so many penny stock brokers. But, with so many penny stock brokers out there, how can tell which ones can give you the best quality of service? Here are the criteria to look for:

Transaction fee

This refers to the cost of trading, which is usually imposed per trade that you make. The amount of transaction charges can be a bit tricky. Some brokers offer a lower transaction fee only as a promo to get you sign up on the site, but then impose a more expensive rate after the promo period.

Surcharge

This is a small amount usually imposed on every share that is under a dollar, while some impose it for shares under $3, depending on the broker. Although surcharges are usually very little, you should be mindful of them because they pile up quickly. For example, if you have 100,000 shares with a $0.01 surcharge for every share, you will have a total surcharge of $1,000. Also, when you trade penny stocks, you will usually have to buy lots of stocks in order to get significant profits.

Trading restrictions

You should be able to trade and manage your account on your own. This means that the platform should not require you to call or send a message just to make a trade. You should be able to trade on your own with a few clicks of a mouse, without having to ask for any permission from the broker. Do not worry; this should not be a problem, especially when you choose to work trustworthy and well-established brokers.

Volume restrictions

Do not choose a broker that imposes a restriction as to how many shares you can trade or would impose a high charge for a trading a high volume of penny stocks. After all, you will have a high surcharge fee when you trade in a high volume.

Trading frequency rate

As already mentioned, there are brokers that impose a small transaction fee per trade. Although there is nothing wrong with it, some brokers will impose a higher rate of transaction fee if you fail to trade a certain number of times within a given period, to be specified by the broker. Although this would not be a problem if you trade on a regular basis, this can be an issue if you only trade sporadically.

Minimum deposit requirements

The required minimum deposit before you can start actual trading varies from broker to broker. Most platforms will require you to deposit around $100-$250 before you can trade. If you just want to test the water and think that the amount is too high, you might want to try depositing using bitcoins. A bitcoin is a cryptocurrency, and most sites that accept bitcoins also accept a very low minimum deposit provided that you use bitcoins.

Mobile trading

Ideally, you should be able to manage your account and make a trade simply by using your mobile phone. This will allow you to trade anytime and anywhere without having to use a computer.

Rating and reviews

Before you sign up for an account with any trading platform or broker, you should first examine the broker's rating, as well as the reviews left by other traders. Take note of the dates of the latest reviews. If the last reviews are dated about a year ago, then be cautious even if the last reviews are positive reviews. To increase your chances of having a good experience, only deal with legitimate brokers.

Banking

You need to take note of a broker's banking features. You must be able to deposit and withdraw your money easily and quickly. Also, many brokers offer more deposit options, but only have limited options for making a withdrawal. This part is very important to take note of; otherwise, you run the risk of not being able to withdraw your money.

Withdrawal fee

This is a small amount imposed by your broker each time you make a withdrawal.

Create an account

In order to trade penny stocks, you need to sign up for an investment trading account with a penny stock broker. Registration is fast and easy. Not all brokers are the same, so make a comparison of the brokers and choose the one that will best suit your needs.

Here is a list of famous platforms that you check. Take note that this list is not exclusive and there is no guarantee as to their quality of service. This is because the management team and strategy can change from time to time. A good broker today may be the worst broker tomorrow. Also, keep your eye on new and upcoming brokers.

- Charles Schwab (www.schwab.com)

- E*Trade (us.etrade.com)

- TradeKing (www.tradeking.com)

- Interactive Brokers (www.interactivebrokers.com.hk)

- Scottrade (www.scottrade.com)

- TD Ameritrade (www.tdameritrade.com)

- OptionsHouse (www.optionshouse.com)

Demo play

Most platforms offer free virtual credits for a demo play. Although this will not make you earn any real money, a demo play is good to have a taste of what trading is like before you use any real cash. A demo play can also be used to test your strategy. Hence, it is a good way to help cut down your losses.

Start small

Whether you have funded your account with a huge amount of money or not, starting out small is strongly recommended, especially for beginners.

Many traders rush and wager a big amount, so they can earn high amounts of profit. Unfortunately, to increase your chances of success in trading penny stocks, you need to exert serious efforts, research, and even experience. Actual trading is different from what you read in books. Books can merely describe what trading is like, but actual trading is more challenging.

Increase your success rate

Regardless which strategy in the first book that you intend to use, you can increase your rate of success by observing the following pieces of advice. The proper way to apply the following is by actual application.

Fundamental analysis

This is the same strategy used in binary options. Take note that the graphs that you see on your computer are not the actual penny stock market. They are, in fact, the result of what takes place in the actual market. When you do fundamental analysis, you need to analyze the businesses themselves, the economy, the news, and other things that can have an impact on the prices of penny stocks. It is important to focus on the companies because the success of the companies also reflects the price movements of their penny stocks. If a company is doing well, the prices of its penny stocks will also tend to increase.

Limit your orders

Set a limit order so you will not have to keep watch on your computer every minute just to monitor the prices of penny stocks. This also applies both when you make a buy order as well as a sell order. In case of a buy order, limiting your order will help you avoid overpayment. In case of a sell order, this will make you sell your stocks automatically provided your selling price is accepted. Of course, if your set price is not reached, you still keep your stocks and try again.

Stop-loss limit

A stop-loss limit is an effective to prevent you from chasing your losses. Take note that the proper way to apply a stop-loss limit is by setting it before you even commence a trade, regardless whether it is a buy or a sell order. Also, remember that the penny stock market is highly volatile that having a stop-loss limit can be considered a must. So, how does it work? Say, for example, you set a limit of 35%, if the value of your stock drops and reaches 35%, you should accept your losses and make a sell order. Although it is not uncommon to see the prices of penny stocks increasing and decreasing, it is also usual for their prices to experience a dramatic and continuous increase in price. And, many times, continuously clinging to a losing stock, especially if the circumstances show a glaring loss, is the worst decision you can make.

Keep your profit

It is important that you cash out. Yes, sell and cash out. Remember that the only way that the profits on the screen can really mean something is only when you turn them into real cash. As long as they are only on the screen, they are just numbers and are only like the credits that you use when you do a demo play.

Of course, you do not have to cash out everything. A good way is to set a certain percentage, for example, 10% of every successful trade. This means that you will cash out every 10% of each successful trade that you make. This is also a good way to cut down your losses.

Focus on the numbers

No matter what everybody says, the only thing that matters is the numbers that appear on the penny stock market. So, focus on the numbers. Even if a particular stock is being heavily promoted, if you do not see any change in value, you should not consider it a good investment. Also, words can easily be twisted, especially during a marketing hype. Numbers are harder to manipulate.

Reassess your strategy

There is one thing that strongly characterizes the penny stock market: change. Therefore, you need to reassess your strategy from time to time; and see to it that your strategy matches up with the market changes. The high volatility of penny stocks cannot be underestimated, and the changes that it makes have a strong impact on your investment.

Lighten your position

If the value of certain penny stocks experiences a good increase but you notice that the stocks are no longer being promoted or that the news about them has stopped, you should lighten your position by selling your stocks before their value decreases. If there are reasons to believe that their price will continuously increase, then you can just cash out a percentage of those stocks, for example, 50%.

Learn from your mistakes

Mistakes are a normal part of trading penny stocks. In fact, even the real experts still commit mistakes from time to time. Although committing a mistake is normal, doing the same mistake all over again is wrong. Always learn from your mistakes. Make sure you learn them. Also, do not beat yourself hard when you make a blunder. The important thing is that you learn. And by learning, you become a better trader.

Develop your strategy

Since the penny stocks market does not stop to move and change, you need to develop your strategy. A real strategy is a life-long journey. Your strategy must be flexible enough to adjust to the rapid changes in the market, and it must be effective enough to reap decent profits.

When to buy

There are two things about buying penny stocks: 1. which penny stocks to buy; and 2. the price. Ideally, you should make a buy order not simply when the price is low, but the important thing is that the price will experience a significant increase. To find out the best stocks to invest in takes a serious amount of research and study, time, and practice.

When to sell

This is the process of turning those profits into real cash. This is the way to enjoy your profits. It is suggested that even before you commence a trade (buy or sell), you should already know what to do with the stocks concerned. For example, say you have a target profit of 30%. Once your penny stocks increase their value and reach the said target percentage, you should immediately make a sell order. This advice is strongly recommended, especially for beginners. It is worth noting that many traders who lose their investment do not just lose their money because of picking the wrong stocks. In fact, they lose their money because they pick the right stocks but hold on to them for too long — so long that the value of the stocks drops significantly. Again, do not underestimate the high volatility of the penny stock market.

Of course, if circumstances strongly show that it would be a better decision not to make a sell order, then this is something that you should consider. To come up with a good decision, you need to update your research. Of course, the chance of earning bigger always comes with a risk. This option is not advisable for beginners. Beginners should aim for small and regular profits.

Stock split

A stock split is a good sign. This is where the company splits its every share. Therefore, each share will become two shares. For example, if you have 100 shares, a stock split will turn your shares into 200. Of course, the price will also be split. Example: if each penny share is priced at $1, the value will just be $0.50.

A stock split is a good sign. In fact, it is a good strategy to make a buy in immediately when a company declares a stock split. This is because a stock split usually means that the business is doing well. It is resorted to when the shares of the company have already achieved a significant increase in value that it has to split its stocks to come up with more shares that have a lower value. Most of the time, and if the company is able to maintain its excellent performance, the value of the new stocks also increase within a short period of time.

Beware of the reverse split

Unlike the stock split, the reverse split is a bad sign, and you should stay away from it. Usually, companies resort to a reverse split when struggling to survive. As the name already implies, it is stock split in reverse. Example: Every 10 shares that you have will be considered a single share. Consequently, their values will also be added together. This is an attempt to make a company look like an attractive investment. Since the stocks are combined, it will appear to investors that the stocks of the company have increased in value significantly. Although, the truth is that the increase in price is not because of any legitimate flow of income, but the stocks are merely combined and manipulated to make them look like an attractive investment.

"Buy the rumor, sell the fact."

This is a common saying known to stock traders. One of the things that happen in the market is that when there is an upcoming big event, rumors spread easily and quickly. This draws so much attention in the penny stocks concerned, which usually result in an increase in their price. When traders see this, they make a buy order knowing that their price will increase dramatically. The obstacle here is that on the day of the event itself, instead of having a good increase in value, the price begins to drop — and it can be a big continuous drop.

Although this looks bad, it can also be profitable. What happens here is that the rumor makes the value increase so much way beyond the actual increase that the event can bring. But, as you can see, the price of the stocks concerned really increases. So, what you can do is to buy the stocks immediately while they are still low, and sell them right before the event or before their value drops.

Chapter 5: Common Pitfalls and How to Avoid Them

There are pitfalls that beginners and even intermediate penny stock traders always fall for. The way to avoid these pitfalls is to be aware of them and to make the necessary adjustments in order to prevent them from happening.

Insufficient research

When it comes to trading penny stocks, research plays a very important role. This part is what differentiates trading penny stocks from gambling. Of course, if you do not exert the right amount of research, your decisions will be as good as relying on pure lack, which turns you into a gambler. Fundamental analysis is important if you want to increase your chances of earning a profit from a trade. Technical analysis or a study of graphs and charts are also helpful.

Just a hobby

If you want to approach trading penny stocks as a mere hobby and are not willing to make the necessary research, you would do better just by doing a demo play. Most of the time, those people who take this course a mere hobby only lose their money. To have continuous success trading penny stocks, you need to exert serious efforts, study, analysis, and practice.

Forcing a trade

Many investors make a trade simply because they see available funds in their account. Worse, they commence a trade even when surrounding circumstances do not show any promising outcome. Remember that when you trade, it is because there is a good potential to make money out of it. After all, you are not required to make any trade. So, if you do, make sure there is a good reason for it.

Inconsistent

Many traders fail to stick to their original strategy. Because of this, they could not tell whether or not such plan is good or not. Worse, they substitute a worse strategy in place of the original strategy. This usually happens when they see a sudden decrease in the value of their penny stocks. As much as practicable, you should stick to your plan so you will be able to measure just how effective it is. Of course, if the circumstances show that continuing with your strategy will only guarantee a loss of investment, then you can abandon your original strategy, but be sure to come up with a better one. This means that you will have to research again and test your next strategy.

Concentrating on good products

There is a difference between good products and right products. The right products that you should invest in are those whose value will increase. Good products do not always guarantee that the prices of stocks will also increase. After all, a business is not just made of good products. For a business to succeed, it also needs a strong and effective marketing plan, a reliable workforce, trustworthy suppliers, as well as a good public image, among others.

Pump and dump scheme

Pump and dump often happen. Even those who are aware of the pump and dump scheme still fall for it. The reason is because it is difficult to identify, especially if it is done by an "expert." This is another reason why you should develop your own understanding of the penny stock market and make your own decisions.

Short and distort scheme

This is also pump and dump but in reverse. This happens when a person borrows stocks and then sells them. After the sale, he spreads bad rumors about the stocks that he just sold. This will cause the value of those stocks to drop. When it drops, he then buys the stocks at a low price. In today's age where you can easily spread a message to the whole world with a click of a mouse, this scheme is as effective as the pump and dump. It has been used by hacks and fraudsters effectively.

Following expert advice

The problem here is that many "experts" often oversell their expertise. In fact, you can find many "experts" who have more losses than profits. So, be very careful. Also, some of these "experts" operate a pump and dump scheme. It is good to be aware of expert advice, but it is more important that you learn to come up with your own decision. After all, even the real experts also experience bad trading days.

Greed

Greed is one thing that gamblers and traders usually have a problem with, which causes them to lose their money. Greed is deceiving because it appears reasonable. For example, why would you sell your penny stocks right after a 40% increase in value when you can expect it to grow even up to 100%? The thing is, many times, after the said 40% increase, it is followed by a big drop. The 100%, although possible, may never happen at all. This is why beginners you should stick to small and regular profits. You have to focus on increasing your rate of success. Continue to develop your strategy. After all, once you have an effective strategy with a high rate of success, you can always increase the amount of stocks that you trade.

Sticking to known strategies

The real experts study the known strategies and develop their own. After all, up to this time, there is no known strategy that can guarantee a profit.

Although these known strategies can help lower your losses and increase the potential of making a profit, they do not guarantee a positive outcome. Also, the penny stock market continues to move and grow, it is only right that your strategy should also continuously develop and improve.

Investing more after a series of losses

Some people think that since they have lost several times in a row, the next trade will bring them a positive result. This is wrong. The penny stock market does not have a 50-50 probability, and the result of the next trade does not depend on the result of your previous trades. Every trade is unique and requires a separate research and analysis to succeed.

Wrong timing

When certain penny stocks gain popularity and their price increase, some traders join the trend expecting to reap a high profit. The problem here is that right after a big increase in value, it can be followed by a significant decrease. Therefore, if you ride the trend too late, you will only lose your money.

Losing control

There are 3 ways to lose control: First is when you encounter a bad loss. It becomes tempting to chase after your losses. Second is when you get a good amount of profit. It becomes tempting to increase your target profit by investing more; and third, is when you barely gain or lose anything. Simply stated, every trade offers an opportunity for you to lose control and fail to stick to your plan. Having a journal will help you stick to your plan no matter what. Also, if you find it too tempting, just turn off your computer or mobile phone to prevent you from making a very risky trade.

Wrong understanding of volatility

Many traders think that volatility is something that balances itself in the long run. Meaning, after a big decrease in value, it will be followed by a massive increase after some time. Therefore, what they do is to place an investment right after a significant decrease in value of certain penny stocks. The problem here is that the volatility of penny stocks does not have a balanced nature. Even after a drop in price, it can still be followed by another dramatic decrease. In a positive light, a significant increase in value can still be followed by a continuous increase in value. Therefore, doing your research is very important. There are factors that affect the volatility and movement of penny stocks. If you analyze these factors, then you will be one step ahead.

Averaging down

Averaging down is when you buy particular stocks as their value decreases. This assures that you get to buy the stocks at a lower rate each time. This means that once their price finally increases, especially if more than the value at which you first bought it, all those stocks will make you give profits. Although this looks like a good strategy, this also means that you are in possession of a losing stock. If the said price increase does not happen, you will lose a lot of money. And, in the world of penny stocks, it is no surprise to see the price of a certain stock to continuously decrease uncontrollably. So, instead of averaging down and hoping for a positive outcome that may never happen, learn to identify the best penny stocks by doing a good amount of research and analysis of various businesses.

Conclusion

Thank for making it through to the end of this book, let's hope it was informative and able to provide you with all of the tools you need to achieve your goals whatever they may be.

The next step is to put everything into actual practice. So, open an account today with a trusted and reliable broker, begin trading, and rake in serious profits.

Finally, if you found this book useful in any way, a review on Amazon is always appreciated!

CPSIA information can be obtained
at www.ICGtesting.com
Printed in the USA
LVHW090745280121
677402LV00033B/141